THE GOD NAMED HALLOWED

THE GOD NAMED HALLOWED

John Killinger

The Lord's Prayer for Today

Abingdon Press
Nashville

The God Named Hallowed

Copyright © 1988 by Abingdon Press

This book is printed on acid-free paper.

Library of Congress Cataloging-in-Publication Data

KILLINGER, JOHN.
    The God named hallowed.
    1. Lord's prayer. I. Title.
BV230.K48   1988   226'.9606   87-15905

ISBN 0-687-15200-3 (alk. paper)

Scripture quotations are from the Revised Standard Version of the
Bible, copyrighted 1946, 1952, © 1971, 1973 by the Division of
Christian Education of the National Council of the Churches of
Christ in the U.S.A., and are used by permission.

MANUFACTURED BY THE PARTHENON PRESS AT
NASHVILLE, TENNESSEE, UNITED STATES OF AMERICA

For Walt and Eleanor Vernon—
dear friends in life and ministry

CONTENTS

THE GOD
NAMED
HALLOWED

INTRODUCTION

More than anything else Jesus left us, the Lord's Prayer stands at the heart and center of all his teachings. It is without doubt the most effective summary of Christian theology ever given. Consider the topics it covers: the Fatherhood of God, the holiness of the Father, the coming of the kingdom, provisions for those who receive the kingdom, amnesty for all wrongdoing, and deliverance from the Evil One. What more could be said? Oh, there is nothing in the prayer about love, of course; but the one who taught it to us was the Good Shepherd about to lay down his life for the sheep. No, the prayer is a complete statement. It covers every necessary aspect of New Testament theology.

As Joachim Jeremias has amply demonstrated in *The Prayer of Jesus*, the Lord's Prayer is not as thoroughly original as we once believed. It shows many affinities to the prayers of other rabbis in Jesus' day.

But that is no serious detraction from the value or meaning of the prayer. On the contrary, it reflects the prayer's centrality to the line of classical deliverance theology in Israel. We must never forget that Jesus did not spring upon the religious scene without forerunners or preparation. He came in what the Great Apostle called "the fullness of time," when both historical understanding and social events were ripe for his coming. Many sincere teachers were doubtless articulating views similar to those he presented. It remained for him to voice them definitively and to seal them for all time with his dramatic death and resurrection, and by his return in spirit to the company of his followers.

Notre père, qui est en ciel . . .
Unser Vater im Himmel . . .
Lay Cha chúng tôi ở trên trời. . .
Padre nuestro que estás en los cielos . . .
Fader vår. du som er i himmelen . . .
Ojcze nasz, któryś jest w niebie . . .

Think of the hundreds of tongues in which this prayer arises to the Father every day. There is surely no language on earth in which it is not said.

And it is impossible, considering the prayer's vast popularity, that there should be a single moment, at any time of any day or night, when it is not being repeated somewhere, in Spanish, in Chinese, in Swahili, in Maori, in all the languages on earth.

What a pleasant jumble of voices it must seem from the perspective of heaven—a great choral symphony rising from God's saints around the world. And what an incomprehensible feat it must be achieving, of bringing the kingdoms of this world that much closer to becoming the kingdom of our Lord!

How important it is, given the centrality of this

prayer to our faith and the unity it provides among the varied tongues and liturgies of the nations, that each Christian understand the meaning of it as truly and completely as possible. For it is no magic formula, no mere shibboleth designed to convert our souls by repetition without understanding or commitment. On the contrary, it is only as we understand and say it with real intentionality that it begins to perform its vital service in our own lives and to reach out, through our converted attitudes, to others.

Every follower of Jesus ought therefore periodically to restudy the Lord's Prayer, and to reconsider the measure of his or her commitment to its tenets. The prayer ought to be the focus of Lenten and Advent studies, or studies at other times of the year. Preachers should devote sermons to it. It should continue to be the subject of books and treatises in every age, as each era seeks to reinterpret it in the light of new scholarship, new insights, and new social situations.

This book is my own attempt to rethink the Lord's Prayer with my congregation during a Lenten season. I was astounded, as I got into the series of presentations, at the unabashed hunger people displayed for fresh insights into the phrases of a prayer they had been offering nearly all their lives. Their eagerness for each new sermon inspired me, quite frankly, to discoveries I might not otherwise have made.

There are depths upon depths, and I have only scratched the surface.

JOHN KILLINGER

OUR FATHER—
THE *REAL* ONE

"Our Father who art in heaven . . . "

"Our Father."

It is impossible, if one reads the Gospels carefully, to imagine prayer apart from the Fatherhood of God. Again and again the word "Father" drops from the lips of Jesus. His entire practice of prayer was rooted in a sense of intimacy with God as his heavenly Father. Thus, when he taught his disciples how to pray, he inevitably began with the words "Our Father." He himself never prayed, in the pages of the New Testament, without addressing God as Father. He apparently never thought of prayer apart from the Father-Son relationship.

This becomes even more interesting when we realize how Jesus felt about earthly father-son relationships. A little later in the Sermon on the Mount (in which, incidentally, the fullest version of the Lord's Prayer appears), he was talking about asking and receiving from God. "What man of you," he said, "if his son asks him for bread, will give him a stone? Or if he asks for a fish, will give him a serpent? If you then, who are evil, know how to give good gifts to your children, how much more will your Father who is in heaven give good things to those who ask him!" (Matthew 7:9-11). "You . . . who are evil." Imagine that! We hope

that Jesus meant that earthly fathers are en-
meshed in a world that is often evil and ungodly.
But even so it is a sweeping indictment. Earthly
fathers, he seems to have been saying, are severely
limited by their nature or environment.

Now add to this another saying. Jesus was
discoursing about the scribes and Pharisees, who
loved earthly authority. He described them in no
uncertain terms as men who did almost everything for show and personal praise, and advised
his followers not to be like them. "You are not to
be called rabbi," he said to his disciples, "for you
have one teacher, and you are all brethren"
(Matthew 23:8). That is, they were advised not to
seek titles for themselves, but to be content to
dwell together as brothers or equals. Then this:
"And call no man your father on earth, for you
have one Father, who is in heaven" (Matthew
23:9).

Did Jesus attempt systematically to alienate
his followers from their earthly fathers? What
was he hoping to do?

The answer lies in the Hebrew concept of the
father. The father was the dominant figure in his
child's life, and the one through whom "the
blessing" passed to the child. The father's
blessing was considered very important. Who can
forget the story of Jacob and Esau, and the way
Jacob tricked blind old Isaac, his father, into
giving him the blessing that by the rights of
primogeniture should have gone to his elder
brother, Esau? Jacob would have done almost
anything to secure the blessing, and then Esau
almost killed Jacob for having gotten it. For a

father to bless a son meant that the son would live happily and prosperously the rest of his life. Of course it was primarily a psychological matter, a state of mind; but who would gainsay the importance of a state of mind, or its role in determining a son's destiny?

Maybe you haven't considered it, but the idea of the father's blessing still has a lot of significance today. A friend of mine was telling me about a book he had read on the subject and what it meant to him. "I realized," he said, "that I have gone through life looking for the father's blessing I never received. It is the one big thing missing from my life. I am restless and dissatisfied because I never felt I had it. And now my father is dead and I shall never have it."

I have heard women say the same thing, that they were frustrated in life because they had never been blessed by their fathers. Their fathers had never given them the full assurance of their love and good will. They had never held them and said, "I love you and I bless you."

As odd as it may seem, it is not enough for the mother to do this. The father must do it. The relationship to the mother is different. It is organic. She carries the child in her womb, nurtures it there, bears it, and then nurtures it again. The father is a kind of "intimate outsider" to all of this. It is his sperm that first calls the child into existence, but then the mother takes over the real support of the embryo and the child it produces. The father's relationship becomes primarily psychological, not physical. And it is perhaps for this reason that the psychological blessing of the father is always so important to the child. The child that doesn't receive the blessing, or *thinks* he or she doesn't receive it, hungers for it for a lifetime.

But Jesus knew the state of the world, the way things are. He knew that human fathers are unreliable at best, and that even if they do give their blessings these are not always enough.

The poet Tennyson's father lived a miserable existence because his father had bypassed him and settled his estate on a younger brother. Even though he became a clergyman, he drank excessively all his life and quarreled constantly with his wife and children. He was tormented by the thought that his father disliked him and preferred his brother.

A woman I knew in Paris, France, had left home at an early age because she did not feel that her father loved her. In her thirties, she suffered from acute depression and malaise. She traveled back to the States, had a tearful reunion with her father, and came back much elated at his assurance that he had always loved her, though he had difficulty expressing his emotions. "Still," she said, "I will never be the woman I might have been if I had only grown up with this assurance. I am already marked for life."

And what of those who have always had the assurance, whose fathers have taken the care to bless them from the beginning?

Sam Keen, the author-theologian who is an editor of *Psychology Today* magazine, answers this question. His father did bless him. They always had a wonderful, secure relationship. Sam remembers "how warm and friendly the nights of childhood were" because his father had a great, booming voice that could hold at bay the very hounds of hell. After his father died, Sam traveled home from the West Coast to the little town in East Tennessee where he grew up, and while he was there he began to weep. He himself was now middle-aged, and he cried,

Father, Father, who does not want a strong and wise protector? Who is so grown up as to have lost the desire for protection against the terrors of the night? The beasties and things that go bump don't wear the faces of bears or burglars as we get older. They all begin to wear the mask of death. And in the presence of that old man we flock to Master-Father-Guru-God who promises us protection. (*Beginnings without End* [New York: Harper & Row, 1975], p. 34)

Not even the blessing of a good earthly father is enough.

Jesus understood this, and that is why he counseled his followers, "Call no man your father on earth." He wasn't against fathers. He merely knew their inadequacy. He knew that no earthly father can love enough and give enough to suffice for all our needs, at every moment of our lives. Only the heavenly Father is equal to this.

For Jesus to call God our heavenly Father was to make the most audacious theological statement that could ever be made. Think about it—the God who created the world and cast the nebulae in space; the God who heard the prayers of the first man and woman on earth and who sees the intricacies of the future; the God whose

19

majesty is seen from the highest mountain and who inhabits the jeweled depths of the darkest ocean; the God who led the Hebrews out of captivity in Egypt and spoke when Jesus was baptized, saying, "This is my beloved Son, listen to him"—*our Father.*

The God who fashioned the giant sequoia tree and plants the tiny seeds of pearls in all the oysters; the God who called Abraham from Ur of the Chaldees and made Saul of Tarsus an apostle to the Gentiles; the God who imprisoned energy in coal and whispered the secret of relativity into the ear of Einstein—*our Father.*

The God who set the oceans rocking and shaped the crescent beaches of distant islands; the God who blessed the world with language and then confounded it with many tongues; the God who ordained the very existence of mortality and then raised up Christ from the coldness of death—*our Father.*

If it doesn't make shivers run up and down your spine, then you have not properly understood. To think that the God of all this depth and power and resourcefulness should be our Father, the one with whom we are privileged to live in an attitude of intimacy and relationship, is enough to stagger the mind, to make it recoil through sheer insufficiency. "Our Father." It is confession, praise, triumph, unbelievable fortune, overwhelming good news! Who could ever have hoped or dreamed that the God of the universe, the God of *all* universes, should be *our Father?*

It was a favorite trick of the old novelists and playwrights, ages ago, to spin their plots around some luckless and penniless boy or girl, adrift in the world without friend or status, who in the end discovers that he or she is the long-lost heir of a fabulously wealthy father who has been searching everywhere for his child through long and lonely years. And well it was a favorite trick, for that is the story at the heart of all humanity, the story our Savior has taught us, that we are the long-lost children of God, and that all we have to do to turn our fortunes around completely is to say "Our Father" and embrace him as one who has searched for us down the years, waiting until we should recognize our relationship and claim it as the gift he has always wanted to give us.

What a difference it makes in the life of prayer! Not believe in prayer? Why, when one realizes he is our Father, one can do nothing else but pray. Not have time to pray? Why, when we have discovered our true relationship to him, we shall want to pray all the time. Not know how to pray? Why, no one has trouble talking or listening to a real Father. When we are able to say "Our Father" and know it and mean it in all sincerity, prayer becomes to us the most natural activity in all the world—far more natural than most of the things we do in the run of a day. Then we would rather pray than eat or sleep or watch television, for prayer is our line of connection to the heavenly Father.

It was so with Jesus. He was always going apart to be with his heavenly Father. Apparently he even forgot about eating and sleeping when he was with his heavenly Father. The power of his life and thought and ministry all came from his heavenly Father. It is no wonder that the disciples—especially John—came eventually to identify him with his heavenly Father. Everything he did had the heavenly Father's stamp upon it.

The real test of his "Our Father" thinking came, of course, on the cross. If he was ever going to decide he was wrong about the Father's care and presence, it was there. No crueler instrument of death ever existed. Talk about a deterrent to crime—the Romans often lined whole roadways with such crosses, to remind the populaces that resistance and insurrection would be met with pitiless torture. When Jesus saw such a death looming before him, he went into the Garden of Gethsemane to pray. Saint Luke says it was his custom. Only this time he prostrated himself and cried out, "O Father, if it be thy will, let this cup pass from me."

"O Father." The heavenly Father. The real Father, one who cared for him beyond any earthly father. The one in whose power he had lived, to whom he had prayed for years. The one who had altered the very course of history, and could alter it now, if he would.

But he didn't. The soldiers came. There was a farce of a trial. The crowd was whipped into a frenzy, crying, "Crucify him! Crucify him!" And, reality of realities, Jesus found himself stripped and laid on a cross, staring dizzily into the cirrus clouds floating overhead as men drove spikes of pure pain into his hands and feet. Where was his Father then? If he was ever going to renounce this Father as a figment of his youthful imagination,

22

as a pious concoction of his religious mind, it was now, as his body was raised on the gallows and his whole life dwindled down to the vanishing point.

But Jesus didn't, did he? "Father," he prayed, "forgive them; for they know not what they do" (Luke 23:34). And then, as he died, "Father, into thy hands I commend my spirit" (Luke 23:46).

A Father to be trusted in death as much as in life.

That's what Sam Keen was looking for, wasn't it? A Father beyond all fathers, a Father who would not die, a Father who would always be there, for ever and ever, world without end.

"Our Father."

The world begins when we can truly say it.

THE IMPORTANCE OF REVERENCE

" . . . hallowed be thy name."

It was Sunday. The family was seated around the dinner table after church. Six-year-old Bobby, lost in thought, was tracing designs in his mashed potatoes with a fork. Suddenly he interjected a serious question into his parents' conversation. "Why don't we call God by his name?" he asked. His parents were puzzled. "What do you mean, dear?" asked his mother. "I mean, why don't we call God by his name?" he repeated. "I don't understand," said his mother. "Well," explained Bobby, "in church we always say 'Hallowed be thy name,' and then we never call him that."

Bobby's question may have more serious implications than we realize. Why don't we call God "Hallowed"? Or, to put it another way, why don't we pay more attention to the holiness or sanctity of his name? We repeat the phrase casually—"hallowed be thy name"—without really contemplating the magnitude of what we are saying. If we actually knew what we were doing—if we were at all sensitive to it—we might well fall silent in wonder and awe!

The ancient Hebrews were extremely cautious about using the divine name, for they believed that even pronouncing it put the speaker in jeopardy. Other tribes and peoples might say the names of their gods as often as they liked, for their gods were not the real God. But to say the name of the real God was like releasing the power of a thousand thunderstorms all at once. Therefore the name Yahweh, the most powerful of all the names of God, was spoken only once a year, and then by the High Priest when he entered the Holy of Holies in the temple.

"Hallowed"—the word means "holy" or "sanctified." But our age doesn't have much sense of the Holy, does it?

A writer of religious books used that phrase, "the Holy," in a book he was writing. When the edited manuscript of the book came from the publishers, he noted that the person who had edited it had drawn a little arrow after the word "Holy" and had penciled above it the word "Spirit." In a telephone conversation with her, he asked why she had added the word "Spirit." "Oh," she said, "I thought you were talking about the Holy Spirit and had left out a word." He explained that he had not omitted anything, that he really wanted to use the expression "the Holy." "But I don't think people will understand that," she said. "We never hear anything about 'the Holy' these days."

It is ironic, isn't it? We speak of God often, with great ease and even occasional irreverence, and yet have little sense of the Holy or the Sacred. Unlike the ancient Hebrews, we even make jokes and funny movies about the power of God. We hawk God in books and magazines and television programs as if he were some ethereal cosmetic or heavenly deodorant. We plaster his name on billboards and bumper stickers. Yet we have little real feeling for the meaning of his name.

There was a recent newspaper article about a gang of youths riding their motorcycles through a local cemetery, toppling headstones, smoking pot, and having sex on the graves. One elderly man who was trying to repair his wife's grave was overheard asking, "Is nothing sacred any more?"

It's a fair question. What is sacred when there is no sense of the Holy? The holiness of God, you see, is like a tent pole holding up everything. When it is no longer there, or when people no longer respect it, there is no reverence for anything.

True reverence is hierarchical, not democratic. It descends from above. When God is honored, all life is sacred. When God is dishonored, nothing is sacred. Oh, we may speak very well of the sacredness of motherhood and the sanctity of a man's word and the dignity of human life. But these become hollow phrases in a world where there is no real respect for God. We cannot have a little bit of holiness in the world. We will either have the holiness of God or have no holiness at all.

We should have known the modern world was in deep trouble in the nineteen-fifties when a young woman in West Germany scrawled across a cathedral door in her town the words "Elvis Presley—My God." At the time, people tittered. It seemed amusing. A fraulein from Germany worshiping a rock star from America. But it was a sign, a symbol of the agnosticism spreading across the Western world. And when that agnosticism was full-blown—when the name of God had been devalued in almost every major city on the globe—we found ourselves plunged into a moral and spiritual morass like none we'd ever known. Our psychological compasses went wild. Marriages began to break up, homosexuality became rampant, there was a surge in violent crimes, the younger generation was lost to drugs and alcohol, pornography exploded everywhere, "me-ism" became a recognized philosophy of life, and international terrorism was born. We can blame it on other things—the haunting possibility of nuclear war, a burgeoning economy, the natural revolutions of postmodern existence. But it is all basically derived from one thing—the loss of a sense of reverence, of a feeling for sacredness, of the conviction that there is a God who cares and has involved himself in human life.

"I don't get no respect," laments Rodney Dangerfield. Neither does anyone else in a world where God's name is not hallowed.

Jesus understood this. It is why he set the hallowing of God's name at the very beginning of the Lord's Prayer, next to the opening address of the prayer.

He knew that the failure to respect God's name lay at the root of all the moral and spiritual problems of his own day. The very context for the Lord's Prayer, in Matthew's Gospel, is a warning against praying emptily and voluminously, as many people did, and an injunction to pray quietly and humbly, aware of the reality and power of God. A people who truly respected the name of God and the power behind the name would not have been spiritually destitute, even though their country was overrun by the Romans. They would not have been blind and deaf to the many signs and wonders of the fullness of time and the coming of God's long-awaited kingdom. They would not have crucified the Savior God sent among them, and persecuted his disciples.

"Pray then like this," Jesus counseled his followers: "Our Father who art in heaven, hallowed be thy name."

In their lives, at least, it would restore order. In their lives, at least, the tent pole would be raised. In their lives, at least, there would be a regaining of perspective and depth and reverence.

And more than that, the new power in their lives would bring order and perspective and reverence to the lives of others as well. The whole world would be changed by the passion of their convictions. Empires would rise and fall around their faith. The map would be altered because of their beliefs. Reverence would become contagious. Because they hallowed God's name, it would be hallowed by millions of people for centuries to come.

Think of the power of a good name to preserve order and justice and joy in a community—any name in any community.

When I was a boy growing up in the small town of Somerset, Kentucky, one of the two senators from Kentucky serving in the United States Senate was the Honorable John Sherman Cooper from Somerset. John Sherman Cooper had a wonderful reputation in his home town. He was loved by both Democrats and Republicans. He was not a dynamic public speaker, and I am sure that is why he never ran for the office of president, but as chairman of the Foreign Relations Committee in the Senate, he was one of the most powerful men in Washington. I delivered the *Louisville Courier-Journal* every morning to his mother's house, and occasionally I saw the great man when he was visiting at home. His power, his honesty, his high idealism, thrilled my childish heart. He brought order and perspective to my world.

Years later, when I was the pastor of a small country church, there was a man in our congregation named Mr. Edward K. Cook. Ed Cook and his wife, Myrtle, were the only two college graduates in the entire congregation, and he was a pillar of the community. If anyone in the region wanted to know about anything, he or she went to Mr. Cook. If Mr. Cook didn't have an answer he always knew where to get one. He was a thoughtful, simple man with great humility and respect for God. And he stood like a colossus in that small community, holding up the sky for everyone else.

Or take an example from history. Following the war between the States, life in the South was often bleak and depressing. But one bright star in its firmament was General Robert E. Lee. The very name gave hope and pride to a vanquished people. When General Lee made a trip from Lexington, Virginia, through North and South Carolina to Florida, his train was met at virtually every stop by thousands of persons wanting to see and touch him. Hundreds of children were pushed toward him on the station platforms bearing notes saying they had been named Robert E. Lee in honor of the great man. Historians say he was regarded as a glorious knight, a king, a god. His very name stood for faith, honor, loyalty, excellence, and goodness.

Now, if an earthly name can mean so much—the name of an eminent citizen or a great warrior—how much more does the name of God mean? God, who called Abraham to be the father of a great people. God, who delivered the Jews from bondage in Egypt. God, who raised up Saul and David and Solomon. God, who addressed Moses at the burning bush and Elijah in his cave and Job through the whirlwind. God, who sent the Messiah. God, who sheltered and shaped the fledgling church. God, who spoke through Augustine and Anselm and Luther and Wesley. God, who is responsible for the rise of modern education and medicine and the missionary endeavor. God, who created and is creating the world.

"Hallowed be thy name." And when it is, the tent pole goes up, order prevails, the world shakes off chaos.

"Hallowed be thy name." And when it is, the soul knows its home.

"Hallowed be thy name." And when it is, our eyes are opened and everything becomes a miracle.

"There is nothing so secular," says Madeleine L'Engle, "that it cannot be sacred, and that is one of the deepest messages of the Incarnation" (*Walking on Water* [New York: Bantam, 1982], p. 50). Of course. It is part of the message of the Lord's Prayer itself.

"Hallowed be thy name."

A man in Dallas, Texas, a real estate broker, told me this story. "I was living life in the fast lane," he said, "condos, horses, drug parties, Ferraris, and Porsches. But it was empty and growing more and more so. Nothing seemed to satisfy me. I tried harder drugs, bigger and bigger business deals, but nothing filled the emptiness. I cursed—oh, how I cursed. Yet my voice just rattled around, like the universe was a house where nobody was home."

Then he met Christ through a woman he was dating, and he learned about prayer and humility and reverence. His life was turned around.

"Now," he says, "I get more thrill out of a candle on our kitchen table than I used to get from all those explosive things. I'm more excited about the song of a bird than I was about all those parties I was going to. Bread tastes better. Sex feels keener. My mind is clearer. Life is richer than I ever knew it could be. I get up every day and say 'Hallelujah!' "

Hallelujah.

"Hallowed be thy name."

It means the same thing. God's name is above everything. It is deserving of honor and glory and praise.

And he is our Father.

THE FATHER'S WILL AND KINGDOM

"Thy kingdom come, thy will be done, on earth as it is in heaven."

What if one day we were all saying the Lord's Prayer and suddenly, after we had said "Thy kingdom come," somebody stepped to a microphone and shouted, "Stop! You don't really mean it!" It would make us think, wouldn't it, about whether we really do mean it. And, the chances are, we don't.

For if we were truly sincere in praying for God's kingdom to come and his will to be done on earth as it is in heaven, it would mean some radical changes in the way we live. Many of us would go to the bank tomorrow and withdraw our money and give it to fight hunger and poverty in the world. Some of us would spend the afternoon going to see our enemies and asking their forgiveness. Others would be thinking about how to reform their companies and businesses to give customers more value and to show more care for the employees and their families. Still others would be thinking how we could redesign our educational system so that it would lead to wholeness and not to fragmentedness and failure. We would all rearrange our daily schedules to include more time for loving one another and worshiping God.

But maybe we have not realized this because we have not understood the meaning of the kingdom.

Reuel L. Howe and his associates at the Institute for Advanced Pastoral Studies in Bloomfield Hills, Michigan, conducted a study a few years ago to learn about lay people's biggest complaints about the church's preaching. One of the major annoyances, said many people, is the meaningless jargon preachers use. Asked what some of this jargon is, they mentioned the words "salvation," "judgment," "redemption," and "gospel" (*Partners in Preaching* [New York: Seabury, 1967], p. 29).

I wonder if the word "kingdom" might not be included in such a list. How much do we know about kingdoms? Few of us have ever lived under a king or queen, and those who have have never experienced the despotism that was once characteristic of rulers. Henry VIII of England stripped a man of his lands and title for laughing at the wrong time. Louis XIV of France imprisoned a man for life because he didn't like his appearance. Tamerlane, the Mongol ruler, destroyed whole cities that didn't please him and erected enormous pyramids of the inhabitants' skulls.

Most ancient peoples lived under such absolute monarchs. When they prayed the words "Thy kingdom come," therefore, it was a prayer for the *antistructure* of God to replace the structures of this world.

To understand the kingdom of God, we should give some thought to God's kingdom as *antistructure*, as the opposite of the way things are. The world under a new Ruler—a divine Ruler—whose thoughts, as Isaiah said, are not our thoughts, and whose ways are not our ways. Everything turned over to God. His will done on earth as it is in heaven.

Imagine that, if you will.

It is not conceivable that anybody in heaven should do anything contrary to the will of God. The angels do his will. The saints do his will. The Son does his will. Everybody does his will in heaven. No exceptions. The *antistructure*. It is not like our world, where very few people do his will, and none do it perfectly.

And if we really mean it, that this is what we want—"Thy kingdom come, thy will be done, on earth as it is in heaven"—then we are asking that radical changes be made, both in our own lives and in the world around us.

The problem is—may I guess it?—the problem is that we don't really believe that the Father's kingdom is at hand and already among us. Isn't that right? Who really believes it is here?

If it is, it is well disguised, isn't it? Secularism rampant everywhere; the world teetering on the brink of nuclear destruction; people grossly materialistic, buying cars and computers and VCRs while a third of the world's population is starving; crime stalking our streets, our corporate life, our political system, like a hairy monster with blood on its hands and mouth. Even our churches are so divided and contentious that one denomination despises another and members put their individual churches above the welfare of all.

The kingdom isn't among us—at least, not very clearly.

We're like the Jews of Jesus' day. They couldn't see it either. They kept talking about the signs of its coming: changes in the heavens, eruptions in the mountains, great shifts in political life.

And Jesus, hearing all of this, countered: "The kingdom of God is not coming with signs to be observed; nor will they say, 'Lo, here it is!' or 'There!' for behold, the kingdom of God is in the midst of you" (Luke 17:20-21).

Imagine that! Already there, and they didn't know it. Growing like yeast in the dough, like a tiny mustard seed quietly expanding to provide a tree for the birds of the air. So close to them that they could reach out and touch it, and they weren't aware of it.

Even John the Baptist had his doubts. When things aren't going right, we all have our doubts, don't we? John was in prison, and he sent some disciples to ask Jesus, "Are you really the one who was to come with the kingdom, or should we look for another?" After all, if Jesus was the one, what was John doing in prison?

What did Jesus answer? Do you remember? "Go and tell John what you hear and see," he said to the messengers; "the blind receive their sight and the lame walk, lepers are cleansed and the deaf hear, and the dead are raised up, and the poor have good news preached to them. And blessed is he who takes no offense at me" (Matthew 11:4-6).

It was the way the prophet Isaiah had said it would be. *Antistructure*, the world turned on its head. Blind people seeing, deaf people hearing, lepers becoming whole again, dead people reviving, and the poor—not the rich, mind you, but the poor—having good news preached to them. A reversal of what the world expects. *Antistructure* beginning to work in the midst of the structures.

Pär Lagerkvist, the Swedish author who won the Nobel Prize for literature, was an agnostic, but ironically he saw what many Christians have not seen. In his novel *Barabbas,* he depicted Mary Magdalene of the Gospels as a poor little harelipped prostitute who is an outcast in society. At night she sleeps among the beggars and cripples and lepers in the valley of Gehinnom, outside the city of Jerusalem. She lies there listening to the moaning of the old. In the distance, she hears the tinkle of a leper's bell. How wonderful it will be, she thinks, when the kingdom comes. She imagines that angels will let down great silken canopies over the entire valley, covering the refuse and decay, and then spread enormous feasts for the poor. But shortly after this she is accused before the elders of being a blasphemer—someone has overheard her saying that Jesus is the Son of God—and she is taken out to a pit to be stoned to death. The old man who accused her is the one to throw the first stone. Soon the entire crowd that rings the pit is hurling stones, and she sinks to her knees, broken and bloody and dying. And what words does Lagerkvist put on her lips? That her dream was a fraud, a mistake? No, "He has come!" she exclaims. "He has come! I see him!"

The kingdom is here—in Christ. It is already

establishing its beachhead—in us. That is why praying "Thy kingdom come" is so radical. It is personal. When we pray it, we are asking that it come in us, that God use us for his beachhead in the world, that his will begin in us and then spread to others.

If we can't honestly pray "Thy kingdom come," it may be because we are satisfied with what we have and who we are, that we don't see any need for change. It may be because we have so much, and are so comfortable with the way things are that we don't want anything to change. We don't want to have to support the poor; we don't want to forgive our enemies; we don't want to reform our companies or redesign our educational system; we don't want to spend more time in loving and worshiping.

Jesus said it is harder for a rich man to enter the kingdom of heaven than it is for a camel to pass through the eye of a needle. He knew, didn't he? When you're on top of the mountain, you don't want the mountains and valleys to be leveled. It's the poor and the blind and the deaf and the lepers and the dying who really pray for the kingdom. The rest of us want it to come, but not now. We want it to come, but not in us. Our structures are so pleasant for us that we don't want the *antistructure* interfering with them.

Shortly after the end of World War II, Helmut Thielicke was preaching to his congregation in Stuttgart. Germany was in ruins, and so was the old church. There was not a person in the congregation who had not been deeply touched by the war. Most had lost their homes, their businesses, their loved ones. Thielicke stood by the altar in his old army boots because he could not get any shoes. He preached on the Lord's Prayer. When he came to the phrase "Thy kingdom come," he asked, "How can these words have any meaning for us, in this wretched condition?" The truth is, he said, we can now understand the need for the kingdom better than we ever could before. Before, our lives were safe, happy, well ordered. They were Platonic and unreal. But now we see how deceptive appearances were. Now the telephone wires are down, the hospitals are bombed out, there is no food or medicine. Now there is just us and God. "The greatest mysteries of God," declared Thielicke, "are always enacted in the depths" (*Our Heavenly Father* [Grand Rapids: Baker Book House, 1974], p. 65).

That's when we most want the kingdom, isn't it? In the depths. That's when the *antistructure* makes sense to us. Until then, we are seldom motivated really to desire it.

Does this mean we must all become poor and blind and deaf in order to say the Lord's Prayer with meaning? Perhaps. At least we must care enough about the poor and the blind and the deaf to ask for the kingdom in their behalf. And we must begin even now to share our lives with them. That, after all, is what the kingdom is about—a community of love in which we all try to do the will of God, the way the angels in heaven do; in which we love our enemies and go the second mile and share everything as if it belonged to others and not to us.

Do you understand what I am saying? Let me show you a picture of it. It comes from a book called *Baskets of Silver*, written by Dr. C. Roy Angell, who was for many years pastor of the Central Baptist Church in Miami. It is about a friend of Dr. Angell's who came to him after Christmas and said, "Roy, I've got to tell you about my Christmas! It was the greatest Christmas I ever had!"

Shortly before Christmas the man's brother had given him a big, new car—a Packard. One afternoon he came out of his office to get in the car and found a dirty little boy, a street urchin, walking around it and touching it and staring at it in admiration. When the man put the key in the door lock, the boy came around to the driver's side and asked him what a car like that cost. The man replied that he didn't know, because his brother had given it to him.

"You mean," said the boy, "your brother gie it to you, and it didn't cost you nothing?"

"That's right," said the man. "My brother gie it to me and it didn't cost me nothing."

The boy appeared lost in thought. "I wist—"he said. The man knew what the boy wished. He was going to say he wished he had a brother who would give him a car. But what the boy said jarred the man all the way to his toes: "I wist," said the boy, "I could be a brother like that."

"What did you say?" asked the man in astonishment.

"I said," repeated the boy, "I wist I could be a brother like that."

The man felt confused and ashamed. He asked

the boy to go for a ride in his car. The boy demurred. He was dirty, he said, and would get the seats dirty.

"You might be dirty on the outside," said the man, "but you're mighty clean on the inside. You will do my automobile good. Get in."

Before they had gone very far, the boy said, "Mister, would you mind driving in front of my house?"

The man smiled, and followed the boy's instructions on how to get to his house. He thought he knew what the boy wanted: to have his family and friends see him getting out of a big car. But again he was wrong. When they got to the boy's house—an apartment in an old brick building—the boy asked him to wait a minute, and disappeared up a flight of stairs. In a short time he came down again, carrying a small boy whose tiny legs hung limply from the hips. He set the boy down on the bottom step, sat down beside him, and put an arm around him. Then he pointed to the car and said, "There she is, Buddy, just like I told you. His brother gie it to him, and it didn't cost him a cent, and some day I'm gonna gie you one."

The man, who had heard this from the car, climbed out and went over to the boys. "So that's the reason," he said, "you wanted to be a brother like that."

"Yes," said the boy. "You see, the store windows are full of pretty things, and I try to remember them, but I can't tell him about them very well, and some day I'm gonna gie him a car so he can see them himself."

"We won't wait until then," said the man. "I'm going to put you both in the car and let you see them today, and I am going to let you pick out anything you want, and I'll buy it for you."

The man did as he promised. And on Christmas Eve, he put up a Christmas tree for them and played Santa Claus. It was the grandest Christmas he had ever experienced (*Baskets of Silver* [Nashville: Broadman, 1955], pp. 96-98).

That, my friends, is what the kingdom is like—acting out the *antistructure* even though we are still in the structures, doing the Father's will as though we were in heaven.

And the funny thing is, when we do it, we already are.

BREAD FOR THE WILDERNESS

"Give us this day our daily bread . . ."

Traditionally, this petition for daily bread has been interpreted as the invocation of a simple lifestyle. There is good reason for such an interpretation. Jesus repeatedly inveighed against the unnatural accumulation of wealth or property. He said that rich people have a hard time getting into heaven. He looked sadly after an attractive young man who would not give up his wealth to become a disciple. He told the stories of the prosperous farmer who died while enlarging his storage barns and the well-to-do city-dweller who woke up in hell because he ignored the beggar asking alms at his gate. And he warned his disciples not to be anxious about what they would eat or drink or wear, because the heavenly Father can be trusted to provide these things in ample amounts.

A prayer for daily bread is very much in keeping with this philosophy of the uncluttered life.

And heaven knows, we need to be less cluttered. When the poet and essayist Emerson said, "Things are in the saddle, and ride mankind," he had no idea how many things most of us would have today. We are the generation that invented the garage sale in order to get a little breathing room. Cars, boats, furniture, clothes, shoes, electronic equipment, household appliances—

they grow like mold in the house, don't they, taking over all the space there is. One woman who had just cleaned out her basement and her attic and was laying the last broken ironing board and stringless tennis racket on the trash pile by the street said, "Now maybe I'll be able to think clearly for a while."

And as for wealth itself, well, the poor probably have no idea how hard it is to be rich, always worrying about protecting that second home from vandalism, fending off salespersons and broker's agents, managing investment portfolios, filling out tax papers, fussing over insurance and retirement and transporting the silverware back and forth from the bank vault whenever there's a dinner party. Peter de Vries, in his novel *Mackerel Plaza* (New York: Signet, 1959), sympathized with all the unfortunate suburbanites who live in a kind of "hand-to-mouth luxury wondering where their next quarterly installment of taxes or the next payment on a third car is coming from." "What I wouldn't give," moaned a prosperous housewife, "to be back in our first little apartment again, where everything was so simple and we slept like babes every night because we had worked hard and played hard and loved each other like the youngsters we were!"

"Give us this day our daily bread." It is no wonder we see it as a clarion call to a life of simplicity, is it?

But, if you will, let me disabuse you of this traditional understanding of the prayer. It is *not* primarily a call for us to return to the simple, unadorned lifestyle.

Jesus, you see, was not an ascetic. Despite everything he may have said about the complications of wealth and property, he was not an advocate of hair-shirt discipleship. John the Baptist was an ascetic, living in the wilderness and eating locusts and wild honey and demanding that his followers abide by a similar regimen. But Jesus, on the contrary, was regarded as a heavy drinker and an overeater. "The Son of man came eating and drinking, and they say, 'Behold, a glutton and a drunkard' " (Matthew 11:19). He went to weddings and parties and dinners in the best homes. He talked about the kingdom as if it were a banquet, not a wake.

Now, what does that do to our traditional interpretation?

The truth is, we cannot divorce the phrase "Give us this day our daily bread" from the part of the Lord's Prayer that precedes it: "Thy kingdom come, thy will be done, on earth as it is in heaven." That is what the prayer is about: the coming of the Father's kingdom. And in the light of that—*because we have asked for that*—we are now to pray for daily bread.

It is a matter of the context.

Do you see the difference? We are not asking for a simple way of life, for a little bread to eat every day—"the enough that becomes plenty." We are asking for the rations we need while the kingdom is being ushered in. "Give us this day our daily bread" is not a summons to asceticism; it is a call to arms!

Let's think back to the wilderness background

of the petition. The story is in the sixteenth chapter of Exodus. God had led the Israelites out of Egypt into the wilderness that lay between Egypt and the Promised Land. When they left Egypt, they had no idea how stark and barren the desert was. Once they were out there and committed to it, their biggest concern was to find food. It would take a miracle to keep them from starving to death. But God gave them what they needed. It was called "manna." Every morning when they rose it lay around them on the ground: small white flakes, like coriander seeds, that tasted like wafers made with honey. The description suggests that it may have been the droppings of the tamarisk bushes, which exude a sweetish, white substance that falls to the ground and crystallizes. The people were to collect an omer of manna (about half a gallon) for each person every day, and to eat it that very day. If they did not eat it, it became infested with worms. The one exception was on the sabbath. On the day before the sabbath, they were to gather an extra omer of manna for each person in order to honor the sabbath day by not working on it. And on this day each week the extra manna did not become infested with worms.

The manna or bread thus became a symbol of the people's dependence on God as they marched through the wilderness toward the land that he had promised them.

And this is precisely what Jesus alluded to in the model prayer. Not a sense of personal abstemiousness—living simply, like monks and hermits—but trust in the Father as we march through the wilderness toward the fulfillment of the kingdom he has promised. We are committed to a journey, just as the ancient Israelites were. We are out to take the world for Christ, and everything else is subordinated to that purpose, even our eating and drinking.

When we pray, "Give us this day our daily bread," we are saying, in effect, "Lord, we are ready to march for the fulfillment of your kingdom. Give us our daily rations and send us on our way! Use us to conquer the world!" It isn't a selfish prayer at all, centered on our needs; it is a war-cry, a pledge of support. It is voluntarism at its highest. "Thy kingdom come—and we are ready in your service to see that it does!"

Now there is a place in God's service for simplicity, and in that sense the traditional interpretation of the prayer verges upon its real meaning. The army of God ought never to travel under encumbrances.

In the early years of the war between the States, when General U. S. Grant was attacking Fort Donelson in Tennessee, the Confederate forces were holding him at a standstill. The fort was situated on a bluff one hundred feet high, and there were twenty-one thousand men inside. Sitting on his horse and quietly musing, as he often did, Grant watched two prisoners being led by. He noticed that they were carrying knapsacks, which he thought was odd for men in a battle zone. He stopped them and inspected the knapsacks, and found a side of bacon and large supply of hardtack in them. "These men are trying to escape," he said. "They have rations for a long march, not a fight." He immediately ordered a renewed attack, and the fort surrendered.

The soldiers of God who are really prepared for battle are not worried about stockpiling wealth and property. Everything they have is put at the disposal of the kingdom.

This is really the point, isn't it? Not that our daily bread amounts to very little, but that whatever we have is our daily bread from God and should be used in the Father's service. Even among the disciples of Jesus there were varying resources. Some of them may have been poor, but there were also some wealthy women, according to Luke's Gospel, who traveled with Jesus and helped to provide for the support of his ministry (Luke 8:2-3). Whatever they had was daily bread. It all came from God and belonged to him.

Here is a contractor who earns millions of dollars by erecting housing developments and shopping centers. He has far more than daily bread in the conventional sense of it. But he knows it is all from God, and out of his abundance he gives faithfully to feed the poor and establish clinics for the sick and preach the good news of the kingdom.

Here is a woman who lives in a large house with a swimming pool and a lovely yard, where she entertains governors and senators and other important people. But she is a faithful disciple of Jesus, who knows that what she has is daily bread binding her to the Father, and in the summertime she receives a busload of Indian children from a reservation to live in her beautiful house and swim in her swimming pool while they visit churches in the area to sing and offer their witness to the kingdom.

Here is the owner of a large publishing firm, who lives in a mansion, flies his own airplane, and owns a farm of Arabian horses. His daily bread is enormous. It sparkles and glitters beside that of most of us. But he regards it as a trust to be used for the Father, and, over the years, has had tremendous influence in the building of churches and schools and the extension of Christian charity.

You see, "daily bread" is not necessarily limited to a meager portion. The important thing is that it is from God and is to be used in his service. When we truly pray that his kingdom will come in our lives, it completely alters the way we look upon our possessions. They are no longer ours to use in any way we please. They are reminders of our relationship to the Father. And they are the means by which we help to secure his beachhead in the world.

There is a beautiful picture of this at the very end of the Gospel of John. It is after the Crucifixion and the Resurrection. Jesus appears to the disciples in the early morning mists by the Sea of Galilee, after they have fished all night and caught nothing. *"Paidia,"* says Jesus ("little children"), "let down your nets on the other side." They do, and catch an enormous draft of fish, so heavy that they can't drag the net into the boat.

Perhaps it's an image of the church's evangelism; we don't really bring people to the Father until the Son gives them to us.

And then, after they eat breakfast there on the

shore, Jesus draws Simon Peter aside. Peter has failed, you know. He caved in when Jesus was being tried before the High Priest, and denied his Lord. And now Jesus draws him aside for some special attention—sort of puts his arms around him and reclaims him for the kingdom. Three times he asks Peter, as they walk by the sea, "Peter, do you love me?" And three times Peter answers, "Yes, Lord, you know I do." And each time Jesus says, "Feed my sheep."

It is believed that Jesus asked him three times because Peter had denied him three times, and, with each response, one of the mistakes was wiped off the slate.

But the first time Jesus asks Peter if he loves him, there is a significant addition. "Peter," he says, "do you love me *more than these?*" More than these. The word "these," in the Greek, can have either of two meanings. It can be a masculine plural, meaning "these men"—"Do you love me more than you love these other men?"—or it can be a neuter plural, meaning "these things." Now it is highly unlikely that Jesus was asking Peter to choose between him and the other disciples; Jesus never treated human love as if it were something to be divided and compared in this manner. It is almost certain that he was asking, "Peter, do you love me more than you love these *things?*"

What things was Jesus referring to? They were walking by the sea. The boat lay there at anchor. The net was probably still attached to the oarlocks, with most of the great haul of fish still entrapped beneath the water. It would have been so easy, so natural, for Jesus to gesture in their direction, or even reach out and touch them. "Peter, do you love me more than these—more than the boat and the nets and the fishing trade?" And Peter said, "Yes, Lord, you know that I love you."

"Give us this day our daily bread."

Nothing wrong with boats and nets and fishing. It was the way Peter made his living. He was the big fisherman. But the Father and the kingdom come first. Jesus comes first. And the rest of it is only daily rations—what we need to be followers and servants of the kingdom.

A FESTIVAL
OF FORGIVENESS

*". . . and forgive us our debts, as we forgive our
debtors."*

It began as an ordinary church service, with a
call to worship and a hymn. Everything went as
usual until about halfway through, when a
layman came to the chancel steps to give his
testimony.

"The Lord has been laying something on my
heart," he said. "There's an awful lot of unre-
solved conflict in this congregation—a lot of hurt
and resentment that's been lying around for a
long time. Some of it has been around so long that
we've forgotten what it's there for. But it has been
getting in God's way. We have been limiting God
by our lack of love and forgiveness in this
church."

As the man talked, the minister looked at the
sermon he had prepared. Somehow it didn't fit
the mood that was being created. He folded it and
put it in his Bible. When the man sat down, he
turned to the Sermon on the Mount and quietly
read these words of Jesus: "If you are offering
your gift at the altar, and there remember that
your brother has something against you, leave
your gift there before the altar and go; first be
reconciled to your brother, and then come and
offer your gift" (Matthew 5:23-24).

"I have been struck," he continued, "by Bill's

words. Maybe we do limit God by our lack of love and forgiveness. If we do, it is time to remove that limitation. Today, there's not going to be a sermon. Instead, we're going to have some free time to think about life and to pray and to go to anyone you want to in this room and ask that person's forgiveness for anything standing between you. Then, when we've all had time to do this, we'll have our Communion."

At first it was very quiet. Nobody made a move.

At last, a woman got up from her pew on one side of the church and walked over and sat down by a woman on the other side. She began quietly talking to the woman. Soon they had put their arms around each other and were hugging.

Then a dozen, two dozen people, began moving around. Soon everybody was talking to someone. There was a steady buzz of conversation in the sanctuary. People were holding hands, crying, embracing one another.

It went on for thirty minutes.

Finally, in an atmosphere of love such as few of them had ever experienced, they heard the Words of Institution, celebrated the Communion, and held hands as they sang "They'll Know We Are Christians by Our Love."

Later, someone called it a love feast. Someone else called it a festival of forgiveness. "Festival, nothing," said yet another person, "it was an *orgy!*"

Do you suppose this is what Jesus had in mind when he told the disciples to pray, "Forgive us our debts, as we forgive our debtors"? Was he thinking of the kingdom as an orgy of forgiveness?

One of God's gifts to Israel was the concept of a jubilee year. You can read about it in the twenty-fifth chapter of Leviticus. Every fiftieth year, which of course occurred but once in most people's lives, there was to be a great festival of redemption and renewal among the people. All debts would be forgiven, those who had fallen into servitude would be released, and everyone would be free to return to his original home, regardless of the obstacles that might have blocked the way for forty-nine years.

There is something of this jubilee flavor about the prayer for forgiveness in the kingdom of God. All debts are cancelled. All impediments to fellowship are removed. There is joy and singing as people rush into one another's arms.

"It has happened!" we are saying. "We have entered that blessed state of the heart in which all obligations are forgotten and all debts are forgiven. We no longer hold anything against our neighbors. God's loving-kindness has risen like the tide of the ocean and purified everything on the shores of human existence!"

When Jesus came into our midst as the embodiment of God's presence, it was as the bearer of forgiveness. When a paralyzed man was brought to him for healing, Jesus said, "Son, your sins are forgiven" (Mark 2:5)—*before* he addressed the problem of the man's infirmity. When a woman was led before him and accused of adultery, he said, "Let him who is without sin among you be the first to throw a stone at her" (John 8:7). Throughout his ministry, Jesus associated with sinners—people shunned by the righteous of his day—and treated them as if God had given them complete amnesty. When he died on the Cross, he prayed for the very people who had crucified him, "Father, forgive them, for they know not what they do" (Luke 23:34). His whole ministry was one of forgiveness and acceptance. Wherever the kingdom came, it came as a festival of forgiveness.

Perhaps this is why the Gospels make so much of the failure of Simon Peter. Did you ever think of that? After all, Peter became the head of the early church. He could easily have quashed or altered the record of his denial of the Lord, had he wanted to. But he didn't. If anything, he seems to have gloried in it. He *wanted* everybody to know what he had done and how Jesus had forgiven him. Forgiveness restored him to discipleship. Forgiveness allowed him to become a leader of the church. Forgiveness made a new man of him. Forgiveness changed his eternal destiny, and he wanted forgiveness to become a jubilee in the church. If he could be forgiven for what he did—cursing and denying that he ever knew the Master—then anybody could be forgiven anything and reclaimed for the kingdom of God!

"Forgive us our debts." How badly we need it! How sick and desperate we often are until we have it!

The words spoken in anger.
The hopes dashed.
The lives messed up.
The chances missed.

The years wasted.

We need forgiveness, don't we, the way Peter did, the way the people around the Cross did, the way the dying thief did.

Here is a man who ruined his children's lives, made an absolute botch of them, and now he can't get the thought of it out of his mind. It haunts him even in the middle of the night.

Here is a woman who failed a friend, who didn't have the strength to share with her when the friend needed it, and the friend committed suicide. How can she ever forgive herself?

Here is a girl, an adolescent, whose parents have loved her with every ounce of their being, have given her everything, have protected her and doted on her and surrounded her with care from the day she was born, and now she is a junkie and a tramp and has only begun to realize what she has done, not only to herself but to them. How will she be able to bear it?

How wonderful it is to experience forgiveness deep in the soul, like a festival or an orgy—to know that one's past is covered over and that the future can be fresh and pure and good. And the most wonderful part is that Jesus, who taught us to pray for forgiveness, is the one who died for our forgiveness, "the Lamb of God who takes away the sins of the world."

"Forgive us our debts, as we forgive our debtors." It isn't only *our* faults, *our* sins. The festival of forgiveness includes the faults and sins of *others* as well.

Jesus said we don't have our forgiveness by ourselves. There was a king, he said, who went to settle his accounts. One servant owed him an astronomical sum—an amount that a daily laborer would earn in 150,000 years! The king ordered the man and his family sold into slavery. But the man howled and screamed and begged for mercy, and the king forgave the impossible debt. Then, as he was leaving the court, the man saw a fellow servant who owed him a much smaller amount—the sum a laborer could earn in 100 days—and demanded payment of him. When the servant proved unable to pay, the man had him thrown into prison. Word got back to the king. He called the man and said, "You incredible fellow! I forgave you an impossible debt. Couldn't you have done as much for a fellow servant?" And he threw the man into jail.

"So also," said Jesus, "my heavenly Father will do to every one of you, if you do not forgive your brother from your heart" (Matthew 18:35).

We do not have our forgiveness alone. When we have ours, others must have theirs as well. The kingdom is a festival of forgiveness, a jubilee of cancelled debts—for everybody.

That is the hardest part, isn't it? Forgiving others who have wronged us. Our lives bear the scars of others' sins. Here is a woman who for thirty years has been consumed with hate for the stepfather who raped her. How can she forgive him? Here is a man whose whole life has been twisted by a public beating and humiliation his father gave him as a teenager. How can he forgive his father? Here is a husband whose wife betrayed him in an ugly, heartbreaking affair. It cost him his pride, his friends, his children, even his home. How can he ever forgive her?

It isn't always easy, but we must forgive others as we are forgiven. Otherwise we ruin the festival and inhibit the kingdom. Had you thought of that? We inhibit the kingdom of God.

Let me give you an example. A minister recently told me about a division that occurred in his church. A local Boy Scout troop had been meeting in the church building for several years. Then, after all that time, a certain board member learned that some of the boys were of another faith and some of another race. He threw a royal fit, and soon had other board members upset. First the board and then the entire congregation became divided on whether to allow the troop to continue meeting in their building. The minister tried to make peace but was shouted down at a congregational meeting. "How could we sing and talk about love and salvation on Sunday morning," he asked, "amidst all that animosity?"

You see?

Inhibiting the kingdom.

Impeding the festival.

Marring the jubilee.

What should our lives together be like? I will tell you a story.

There was a twelve-year-old boy in California who witnessed the murder of his father and the brutal rape-murder of his mother. His life seemed ruined. Sent to a state school for boys, he was apathetic and withdrawn, and did poorly in his work. Although he was paraded through the offices of several psychologists and attended numerous therapy sessions, nothing seemed to break through the shield of defenses his young mind had thrown up.

Then, shortly after graduation from high school, he attended a Young Life meeting and heard the testimonies of several young people about the difference Christ had made in their lives. When an invitation was given to accept Christ, he found himself going forward with tears streaming down his face.

His whole life turned around. His personality underwent an immediate change. Where he had been introverted and withdrawn, he suddenly began to make new friends. He applied to a local college and was admitted. After college, he went on to law school. And while he was in law school, he did something that had been building up in him since the night he accepted Christ as his Lord. He made arrangements to visit the man who had killed his parents.

The man was serving a life sentence in the state penitentiary.

The first visit was not a very good one. They were both nervous and had a hard time talking to one another.

But the young man was determined, and went back a second time. The second visit was a breakthrough. "If God can forgive me for the awful hatred I carried for you," said the young man, "he can forgive you for what you have done."

The prisoner was deeply affected by this message. On the fourth visit, he surrendered his heart to Christ. The two men embraced, mingling their tears of wonder and joy.

And a few years later, when the prisoner was paroled, the young man, now an attorney in Modesto, California, helped him to get a job and start a new life.

This, my friends, is the power of Christ and forgiveness. It is a picture of the festival that ought to be going on all the time in our lives, both inside and outside the church. It is the way we ought to treat one another in all our dealings. It is what the Father has willed for us in his kingdom, and what he has given us through his Son.

"Forgive us our debts, as we forgive our debtors."

You might even call it an *orgy* of forgiveness.

HOLDING ON
TO FAITH

"Lead us not into temptation, but deliver us from evil."

In *Barabbas*, Lagerkvist's novel that I mentioned, there is a scene that haunted me when I read it twenty-five years ago and haunts me today.

Barabbas, the brigand whose life was star-crossed with that of Christ, has become a Roman slave, and is transported to Cyprus, where he will work in the copper mines. There he meets an old Armenian slave named Sahak, who is a devout follower of the Messiah. Each slave wears a metal disk proclaiming that he belongs to Caesar. But Sahak has strange markings on the back of his disk which supposedly spell out the name *Christos Jesus*. Although he belongs to Caesar, his real allegiance is to Christ.

Professing that he too wishes to follow the Galilean, Barabbas asks that his disk be inscribed with the name of Jesus. Working secretly down in the copper mine, they scratch upon its reverse side the same markings that are on Sahak's.

But someone overhears and they are reported to the supervisor, who tells the governor of the island. Sahak and Barabbas are brought before him. He questions them about the markings. Sahak says they are the name of his god. The governor reminds him that Caesar is a god also,

63

and warns him that having other gods before Caesar is punishable by death.

The governor questions Barabbas. Does he believe in this god whose name is inscribed on his disk? Barabbas shakes his head.

"You don't?" asks the governor. "Why do you bear his name on your disk then?"

Barabbas is silent.

"Is he not your god?" asks the governor. "Isn't that what the inscription means?"

"I have no god," Barabbas answers at last, so softly that his words are barely audible.

Sahak gives him a look of such despair and pain and amazement that it seems to pass right through him, into his inner self, even though he keeps his eyes averted.

Once more Sahak is questioned. Does he realize the consequences of wearing the name of his god? Yes. "If you renounce your faith no harm shall come to you," says the governor. "Will you do it?"

"I cannot," says Sahak.

The governor orders him to be taken away and crucified.

"Extraordinary man," he says as he looks after him.

Then he takes a knife, and holding Barabbas' disk in one hand, crosses through the name of Jesus.

"There's really no need," he says, "as you don't believe in him in any case."

And he commends Barabbas for being a sensible fellow, and orders that he be given a better job (*Barabbas* [New York: Random House, 1951], pp. 141-47).

For the rest of his life, Barabbas wears the crossed-out name of Jesus.

That is what this prayer is about: "Lead us not into temptation, but deliver us from evil." It is not about minor temptations, those siren voices of flesh and soul that would beguile us from our spiritual disciplines, but about the final test, the very trial of our faithfulness to Christ. It is about the possibility that we shall turn our backs on the kingdom, that having once set our hands to the plow, we shall walk away and leave the furrow broken and unfinished.

For the dreaded possibility is always there, that we too shall end up wearing the crossed-out name of Jesus.

The Greek word for temptation is *peirasmos*. It also means "trial" or "test." It is a word we ought to learn the way we have learned *agape* (love) and *charisma* (gifts) and *koinonia* (fellowship). We ought to sear it into our minds and keep it before us at all times. We ought to fear it worse than death.

Jesus himself experienced *peirasmos*. Following his baptism in the river Jordan, and hearing his heavenly Father say, "This is my beloved Son," he was led into the wilderness for a testing period of forty days. There, we are told, Satan—the representative of evil—tempted him to turn aside from his devotion to the Father and his commitment to the kingdom. He was tempted to turn stones into bread—the appeal to basic appetites. He was tempted to throw himself down from the highest part of the temple and be borne up by the angels—the appeal to religious pride and confidence. And he was tempted to fall down and worship Satan in exchange for an earthly kingship—the appeal to the desire for power and authority.

All three temptations had one thing in common. They were all appeals to let self, and not God, stand at the center of the universe. That is when we always get in trouble, isn't it? When we let self become the center of everything. Jesus overcame *peirasmos* because he kept God steadfastly at the center. And this is why he told the disciples, "Pray that you may not enter into temptation" (Luke 22:40). If they prayed, if they kept their interest focused on God, they would withstand. Otherwise, they were bound to fail.

Do you remember the story of Peter's walking on the water to Jesus? As long as he kept his eyes on the Savior and didn't think about himself or what he was doing, he was all right. But the moment he looked down and saw the water and was reminded of the impossibility of what he was doing, he began to sink.

And poor Judas, of course, succumbed to temptation. Of all the disciples, he apparently remained the most practical and self-sufficient. He was the keeper of their treasury. He was a man of affairs. And when he came into *peirasmos*, in Jerusalem, he became concerned about saving himself. If Jesus was the captain of a sinking ship, then he wanted a life preserver. So he made his little deal with the chief priests, and sold his Lord for the price of a slave. He put self at the center of the circle and left God out. Afterward, when he realized what he had done, he was so remorseful that he committed suicide. He had not been a man of prayer.

The early Christians often faced persecution and death for their faith; these were their forms of *peirasmos*. But for us it often comes more quietly and insidiously, like the dew on the grass that wasn't there when we went out the last time, or the hour that ticked away before we had any idea it had arrived. It comes as *nothing*, like a stillness in the air that we didn't notice until all the plants had died. We merely drift along, like people asleep on a boat, and wake up to find that we have left our faith behind. In a world where we are not imprisoned for our beliefs, and where Bibles lie about for the taking in every hotel room, we simply forget the importance of the Father in daily life, and Christ becomes a stranger to us. The very absence of pressure leads to our forgetting, our not taking it seriously, our falling away.

"I don't know how to explain the fact that I have not been an active Christian," said a man in his forties. "I always went to church as a youngster. In fact, I even considered becoming a minister. But then I went to college and got out of the habit. My wife and I went a few times during the years, mostly at Christmas and Easter. But we moved around a lot, and I was awfully busy in my work, and we sort of let it slide. Not an unusual story, really, but that's the way it happened."

It isn't unusual, is it? "We sort of let it slide." The crossed-out name of Jesus. Or, as the governor said, there was not much point in

67

crossing it out. Barabbas didn't really believe in Jesus, in any case. Not very strongly. Not enough to remain faithful.

We get busy, and forget about praying and reading the Bible and staying close to the Father. There are family things to do—trips and vacations and outings. There are friends to be with—bridge parties and cocktail parties and golfing dates and hunting trips. There are ball games to attend—how many of us will travel as far and as often to attend spiritual gatherings as we will to see basketball games? There is television to watch—hours and hours and hours of it. Life just seems to go by, and before we know it we have lost all contact with Christ and the kingdom. We didn't plan it that way. It merely happened.

Casual temptation, as opposed to *formal* temptation.

Nothing big. Just not making an effort. Not remembering that Jesus said to pray to avoid it, to be delivered from evil. *Peirasmos* we hadn't expected, that sort of caught us before we knew anything about it. *Peirasmos* that ended with our being stuck in the evil, like the fox and the tarbaby, and we couldn't get away from it.

More Christians are lost this way than any other way.

More churches become weak and crippled and powerless this way than any other way. Not because of some gigantic struggle, some dramatic, unforgettable conflict, but simply because they have drifted away from Christ.

I wish I could horrify you about this. It is worse

than a plague or an epidemic. It is worse than a famine. It is worse than a hurricane or a tornado. It is worse than a nuclear disaster.

Seriously.

"Do not fear those who kill the body but cannot kill the soul," said Jesus, "rather fear him who can destroy both soul and body in hell" (Matthew 10:28).

The poet James Dickey understood. He wrote a novel, a modest-size volume called *Deliverance*. *Deliverance* is a mythological picture of what we're talking about. On the surface, it is the story of four city men, suburbanites, who take a canoe trip down a wild white-water river in north Georgia. On the way, two of them are ambushed and one is raped by murderous locals. They make a hair-raising escape, and the rest of the story is about their hazardous trip down the canyon, with one of the locals stalking and shooting at them from above. When they finally reach safety, they cannot even talk about the ordeal. They are delivered—barely—but their minds are scarred for life. What Dickey has really written is a modern morality play. Life itself is like the passage down a wild, primitive canyon, where we are easy marks for the devils along the way. Like these men when they began their outing, we often manage to laugh and sing and pretend we are having fun. But the evil is always there, lying in wait, ready to spring out and devour us. It erupts when we least expect it. A favorite son cracks up his sports car and is paralyzed for life. A fourteen-year-old daughter gets pregnant. A wife or husband betrays us and leaves us for someone else. A neighbor is stabbed in the parking lot of the grocery store. We lose our zest for life and fall into depression. We find out we have cancer. And if we have no faith, if we have drifted away from it and can no longer pray, who will deliver us? Who will help us through the canyon of life?

"Lead us not into temptation, but deliver us from evil."

This is not an anticlimactic petition. Jesus didn't put all the good stuff at the first of the prayer and leave the junk till last. This petition is as important as any in the prayer. "You have acknowledged that God is your Father and prayed for his kingdom to come," says Jesus. "You have prayed for daily rations and forgiveness. Now pray that you will hold on to your faith and never lose it."

I had dinner with a man and woman in a Southeastern city. They were in their late thirties or early forties. He was a manufacturer's representative and she a social worker. She picked me up at my hotel and was running late because she had spent the afternoon with a foster family in another city. She was bubbly with excitement about how well the family was doing with an abused boy who had been placed with them—he had begun to trust them and share things. Sometimes he even laughed.

At the dinner table, we talked about their faith. She and her husband had grown up in nominally religious homes, had attended church, and then had drifted away. He had gone into sales work after college. She had been an airline stewardess, living in New York, then had come back South and gotten into social work. They met and were married in the church, but still had no real sense of divine presence in their lives.

Then one night one of her old friends from high school called up and said three or four girls were getting together. Wouldn't she like to come? She did.

"And you know what we spent the whole night talking about?" she said. "Christ. My friend had had an adult conversion experience, and she wanted to share it with us. She was so excited about her faith that I guess it sort of rubbed off on me. I wanted to feel as happy as she did. So I went home and thought about it. And I prayed and said, 'Lord Jesus, I want to give my life to you again.' Then, a couple of weeks later, there was a big spiritual rally at the coliseum, and I went and made an open commitment and came back and told my pastor."

She looked over at her husband. "Bill didn't renew his faith until a couple of years later," she said.

"I didn't know what I was missing," he said. "But I could tell she had something I wanted too."

I went to church that night, where I was speaking, greatly warmed by their testimonies. I knew it would be easier to preach, with persons like them in the congregation. After the service, someone asked me who I had had dinner with. When I told the person, she said, "Oh, did they tell you she has lupus?"

They didn't. They didn't mention it. I had heard nothing of any troubles in their lives—certainly nothing about this dreaded, mysterious disease that can manifest itself in so many debilitating ways. They were in life's canyon, and the devils had them in their sights. But they were counting on their deliverance, for they knew who their Deliverer is.

"Lead us not into temptation"—into *peirasmos* —"but deliver us from evil."

STANDING IN
THE KINGDOM

*"For thine is the kingdom, and the power, and
the glory for ever."*

I shall never forget the first time we visited
the famous cathedral of Chartres in France. The
old building, under lumpy gray skies, was dirty
and sullen in appearance. The windows looked
dark and dreary. I stood on the sidewalk outside
and felt disappointed. "How can it be," I asked,
"that this is the famous cathedral to which
medieval pilgrims made their way by the thousands? It is a dour old building with no charm at
all!" But as we had come that far we made our
way inside. And I need not tell you of the
transformation in my attitude. It was magnifi-
cent! Even though little sunlight filtered through
the stained glass, the great windows were a feast
for gourmet souls. Never had I seen such rich
assemblages of blues and reds and other colors. It
was as if I had stumbled into the room in heaven
where the deepest hues of the rainbow are made. I
could not believe the beauty, the rare, incompara-
ble glory of the place.

On the inside, the old church was completely
different from the way it appeared on the outside.

Many people have a similar experience with the
Christian faith. From the outside it looks dull,
superstitious, and restrictive; it appears to be

totally lacking in fun and charm and intelligence. But from the inside it is something else altogether—beautiful, majestic, commanding, and utterly fulfilling to the human spirit.

This is the reason for the final phrase of the Lord's Prayer, the one ascribing kingship and power and glory to God for ever and ever. It was not part of the original prayer Jesus gave to his disciples. None of the earliest manuscripts of the Gospels include it, and therefore all of our modern translations of the Bible omit it or consign it to a footnote in small print. Apparently it was added to the prayer by Christian usage in the decades of the church following the death and resurrection of Jesus. It was the response of early Christians to their experience of standing *inside* the faith, *inside* the kingdom for which they had been taught to pray. It was an exclamation of wonder, which they attached to the words of the Master. "Thy kingdom come," they prayed, and then, "Lead us not into temptation, but deliver us from evil." But they were so excited by everything they had seen and felt that they couldn't stop, so they added, "For thine is the kingdom, and the power, and the glory for ever. Amen."

Does it really matter that they were not the words of Jesus himself? We think of Mozart, commissioned when he was ill and in the final months of his life to write a requiem Mass for a citizen of Vienna. Feverishly he composed the opening sections. His coughing spasms grew worse. He wrote the beautiful "Lachrymosa" passage. And then he died, and was buried in a pauper's grave. But his students could not bear that the haunting *Requiem* would remain unfinished and unsung. They studied his notes. They remembered his techniques. They completed the Mass. And today, whenever it is performed, its lyric beauty pays homage to its famous author, its original composer, not to the students who completed it. So it is with the final phrase of the Lord's Prayer. So what if the words were not those of Jesus? They are the testimony of his followers to the truth of his vision and the reality of the kingdom he preached.

"For thine is the kingdom, and the power, and the glory for ever."

There were precedents. That is, the language of the ascription was not uncommon in Judaism and early Christianity. When King David was giving his throne to his son Solomon, he blessed God in the presence of all the people, saying, "Blessed art thou, O Lord, the God of Israel our father, for ever and ever. Thine, O Lord, is the greatness, and the power, and the glory, and the victory, and the majesty; for all that is in the heavens and in the earth is thine; thine is the kingdom, O Lord, and thou art exalted as head above all" (I Chronicles 29:10-11). Many scholars think the phrase in the Lord's Prayer was fashioned from these very words. But it also bears great similarity to these words from Psalm 145:10-13:

> All thy works shall give thanks to thee, O Lord,
>   and all thy saints shall bless thee!
> They shall speak of the glory of thy kingdom,
>   and tell of thy power,

to make known to the sons of men thy mighty
   deeds,
   and the glorious splendor of thy kingdom.
Thy kingdom is an everlasting kingdom,
   and thy dominion endures throughout all
   generations.

And there is even possibly a connection between
our phrase and the moving doxology of the
apostle Paul in his letter to the Romans, when he
says, "O the depth of the riches and wisdom and
knowledge of God! How unsearchable are his
judgments and how inscrutable his ways! . . . For
from him and through him and to him are all
things. To him be glory for ever. Amen" (Romans
11:33-36).

Whatever the source—and it may have been all
of these!—the early Christians were merely
adding to the words of Jesus a sign of their own
agreement and excitement about the kingdom of
God. They had stood on the inside and knew what
the rest of the prayer was all about. They had seen
the kingdom and the power and the glory, and
knew they belonged to the Father. They were only
adding the word of their testimony.

"For thine is the kingdom, and the power, and
the glory."

It was not a careful list. Kingdom and power
and glory all mean more or less the same thing.
They form a sort of exuberant redundancy.
Basileia, dunamis, and *doxa,* in the Greek; "the
kingdom, and the power, and the glory."

Power and glory were often thought of together.
When Jesus described the "last days" for his
disciples, he said that people would see "the Son

of man coming on the clouds of heaven with power and great glory" (Matthew 24:30). When Paul wrote about the death of the body, in I Corinthians, he said: "It is sown in dishonor, it is raised in glory. It is sown in weakness, it is raised in power" (I Corinthians 15:43). And John, writing of the heavenly temple in the book of Revelation, described it as being "filled with smoke from the glory of God and from his power" (Revelation 15:8).

An American woman who survived a terrible hurricane in the Philippine Islands later wrote a description of what she had experienced. "The wind roared like a freight train," she said, "and we seemed to be right on the tracks as it passed over us. First the lights went out and everything was plunged into darkness. Then the roof came off our bungalow and the rain poured in as if it were the ocean. We ran, struggled, crawled to reach an outbuilding. My husband and I were separated, and I fell in a drainage ditch. By then the wind was blowing so hard I couldn't stand up, so I remained there, crouching in the water and trying to stay out of the wind. Toward dawn, I began to make out the shapes of things sailing by in the air—building materials, furniture, whole palm trees torn up by the roots as if they had been matchsticks stuck in the sand. It was glorious, glorious, glorious!"

The power and the glory—and all about the kingdom. It was the kingdom that was at the center of everything, the kingdom that was prayed for, the kingdom that had come.

But let a modern saint speak about the

kingdom. E. Stanley Jones, the great Methodist missionary to India, who was a friend of Gandhi, was visiting Russia for the first time. He was depressed by what he saw and heard. Russia, he felt, was a great prison of the spirit. He needed reassurance. In his quiet time in Moscow, he was reading the Bible, and a verse leapt out of the book of Hebrews and spoke to him: "Therefore let us be grateful for receiving a kingdom that cannot be shaken" (Hebrews 12:28). A kingdom that cannot be shaken—not only *will not,* but *cannot* be shaken. "I saw as in a flash," he said,

that all man-made kingdoms are shakable. The kingdom of communism is shakable: they have to hold it together by purges, by force; they cannot relax that force or it will fall apart. The kingdom of capitalism is shakable. The daily fluctuation of the stock market, on account of the course of events, shows that the kingdom of capitalism is shakable. The kingdom of self is shakable. Center yourself on yourself as the center of your kingdom and the self will sour and go to pieces. The kingdom of health is shakable. The radio and TV blare constantly with supposed health remedies to hold this physical life together, but in the end the grim reaper death gets us all. Everything is shakable, except one—the Kingdom of God, the one and only unshakable Kingdom. (*Song of Ascents* [Nashville: Abingdon, 1968] , pp. 149-50)

This is why the early church testified, "Thine is the kingdom, and the power, and the glory *for ever*"—in limitless, measureless time, beyond all the boundaries of human imagination.

"Just think," said a man to his little boy, "if you

were to begin now to pick up a grain of sand from the beach each hour of every day of your life, and were to continue this action for the entirety of your life upon earth, until the day you died, you would have made only the same effect on the shoreline of this country as if a million years had been removed from the edge of eternity."

"Thine is the kingdom, and the power, and the glory for ever."

It isn't any wonder, is it, that the early Christians were a people of song, or that G. K. Chesterton described them marching to their deaths "as if they smelled a field of flowers afar off"?

That's what we must remember, to appreciate this doxology—that they added it to the words of Jesus at a time when it was hardly safe to be Christian, when their fathers and mothers and brothers and sisters were being crucified or put into prison or thrown into the arena with lions. "Thine is the kingdom, and the power, and the glory for ever," as they were being clapped into slavery.

Which means that we can pray this prayer under any conditions, doesn't it? Even when the company is moving us and we are saying goodbye to a home we have always loved. Even when we are standing in line for an unemployment check. Even when the doctor has told us we have an incurable disease. Even when we are lowering the body of a dear little child into the grave.

"Thine is the kingdom, and the power, and the glory for ever."

At a dinner in Seattle, I met a redheaded young

businessman named Bill McElvaney. I noticed that he limped a bit, and out of rude curiosity asked if he had injured his leg. "It was a war injury," he said. His wife, who was sitting on the other side of him, leaned over and said, "Bill wouldn't tell you, but he was a P.O.W. in Vietnam." Gradually in the course of the next hour I was able to extract part of his story. He had been interned for more than three years. It had been a life of torture and deprivation, during which two things had kept him going: his faith and his family. He had two little girls, one of whom he had never seen, and he thought about them and dreamed about them—about what it would be like if he ever got home, and could lie in bed with his wife in the morning as the girls came into the room and tumbled over them.

Most of the time, Bill said, he was kept alone in a small bamboo cell. It was unbearably hot and humid in the summertime and freezing in the winter. At first he was interrogated almost constantly, but then he was treated with long periods of neglect, when the only person he saw was the guard who set a bowl of soup or rice under the door of the cell. When he was interrogated, he was beaten mercilessly for not providing the information his questioners wanted. "If I had known what they wanted to know," he said, "I'm sure I would have told them; but I didn't know." Yet it was the periods of neglect, when his only company was the lice and spiders, that bothered him most.

"I'll tell you how I stayed sane," said Bill. "I repeated all the poetry I ever knew—all the little bits and pieces we had had to memorize in school—and the Lord's Prayer. I must have said it a million times. I wished I had learned more poems. When I was a boy, I hated Longfellow and Wordsworth, but out there, they became my friends, my saviors. It was the Lord's Prayer, though, that really got me through. I said it backwards and forwards. I said it from the middle to the end and back again. I remember saying it when they were beating me, and I said it at night when I thought I would freeze to death before morning."

"Now when I say it in church," he said, "it reminds me of that awful time I have tried to dismiss from my memory, and I realize how important his kingdom is."

"For thine is the kingdom, and the power, and the glory for ever."

Surely not even Jesus himself could have expressed it better. It is *our* response to what we have experienced of the Father's love and presence in our lives, regardless of what is happening to us in the world. It *is* his kingdom and his power and his glory, and they *will be* for ever. That is the faith on which we stake everything.

AMEN—SO SAY WE ALL

*" . . . the kingdom and the power and the glory
for ever. Amen."*

Several years ago a young preacher was
invited to preach and offer prayers in the chapel
at Vanderbilt University. As the faculty member
in charge of the chapel that day, I was on hand to
greet him. He arrived promptly, but he was not
alone. With him was a diminutive lady whom he
introduced as Aunt Susie. Aunt Susie, he explained, was a member of his church, and she had
come along as his "Amen-corner." She sat near
the front of the chapel, right under the pulpit,
where she could help with the service. All through
his prayers and sermons, she kept up a steady
chorus of "Amen" and "Yes, Jesus." Afterward,
the young preacher said, "I hope it was all right
that Aunt Susie came with me. I could not pray or
preach without her."

In sophisticated circles, Aunt Susie's helping
with the service may seem primitive or even
backward. But she actually reflected a practice
that was central to the liturgical life of the ancient
Hebrews and even of the early Christians. The
Amen was their part of the service. It was the way
they were supposed to respond to the ritual
occurring in their midst.

The first record we have of the use of Amen as

a liturgical response is in the book of Numbers. It is part of the ritual for cursing a woman who has been condemned for adultery. After the priest has pronounced the curse, the woman herself is to reply, "Amen, Amen" (Numbers 5:22). Later in the book of Deuteronomy, the word is again associated with the pronouncing of a curse. This time, Moses is giving instructions to the people about crossing the Jordan River into the Promised Land. Once they are there, he says, the Levites, or priestly tribe, are to pronounce a curse on anyone who makes a graven or molten image. All the people are to answer and say Amen (Deuteronomy 27:15).

In the Hebrew language, the word means "So be it" or "Thus let it be." In its first usage, therefore, it signified a solemn participation in the placing of a curse on someone who had violated sacred law. It was the people's part in a ritualistic action, and expressed their corporate unity in the action being taken.

As such, the word "Amen" has remained the people's assent to worship or corporate action. And, in Christendom's less formal liturgies, such as those in rural areas, it is often freely used to express the people's agreement in what is said.

I remember a large, poorly educated farmer in my first parish. His name was Bud Neely. Bud could barely write his name. He operated what I have since learned to call a "cold-comfort farm," a small plot of ground where he eked out a living with a garden, a few pigs and chickens, and a cow. He shaved once a week, to come to church, and he changed his overalls once a week, for the same

84

reason. I never saw him without a large quid of tobacco in his mouth, except when he was eating; and as soon as he finished a meal he plopped a new quid into his mouth.

Bud said to me once, after a church service in which he had participated rather overmuch, "I ain't much with words, but I can say 'Amen' with the best of 'em."

"Amen" is the people's word.

Sometime after its beginning as a popular response to a curse, this little word that meant "So be it" was elevated to a general covenantal response; that is, it became the way people ratified a covenant between themselves and God, and, we suppose, among themselves as well. When King David decided to place his son Solomon on the thrones of Israel and Judah, he called in Zadok the priest, Nathan the prophet, and Benaiah the son of Jehoiada, and told them what he purposed to do. And Benaiah responded by saying, "Amen! May the Lord, the God of my lord the king, say so" (I Kings 1:36). Benaiah was expressing his agreement with the plan and calling on God to accomplish it.

Even today, the word retains something of this sense of ratification. In a novel called *The Covenanters*, by Elise Manson Barker, there is an old German banker who concludes all of his business arrangements with a handshake and the solemn pronouncing of Amen. And one frequently hears people agreeing with a proposition or a statement by saying "Amen." Sometimes they state it loudly, as a sort of exclamation mark to what has been said, and other times they mutter it quietly to themselves, as though giving private emphasis to something. But it is always a mark of their personal involvement and commitment to a matter.

By the time of the early monarchy in Judah, though, the word "Amen" had evolved primarily into a word confirming praise and honor given to God. In the book of I Chronicles, following a long psalm of praise to God, the writer concludes:

> Blessed be the Lord, the God of Israel,
>   from everlasting to everlasting!
> Then all the people said "Amen!" and praised the Lord.
>
> (16:36)

Nehemiah tells us that when the Jewish exiles returned to Jerusalem and Ezra read to them for the first time from the book of the law, "Ezra blessed the Lord, the great God; and all the people answered, 'Amen, Amen' " (Nehemiah 8:6). And the psalmist, sweet singer of Israel, wrote:

> Blessed be the Lord, the God of Israel,
>   who alone does wondrous things.
> Blessed be his glorious name for ever;
>   may his glory fill the whole earth!
>   Amen and Amen!
>
> (Psalm 72:18-19)

It is easy to hear in these citations foreshadowings of the ending of the Lord's Prayer: "For thine is the kingdom, and the power, and the glory for ever. Amen." The Amen is the personal exclamation point at the end of a phrase paying tribute to the heavenly Father. It is the worshiper's signature at the end of a paean of praise. It is acceptance and commitment and joy all rolled into one. It is the twenty-one-gun salute after the parade of honor.

As such, it is one of the most expressive and powerful little exclamations in the world. And it is all the more powerful for being the same word in every language. Did you realize that it is the one word in the Lord's Prayer that is recognizable wherever one hears the prayer, whether in a cathedral in Paris or a grass hut in Nairobi or an old clapboard church in Mississippi? Stainer's "Seven-Fold Amen" and the Calypso "Amen" from Jamaica never have to be translated in order to move from culture to culture. In every language, they express the sense of joy and unity we feel in the acknowledgment of God as our heavenly Father.

But there is one more thing we ought to note about the little word "Amen." After the death and Resurrection of Jesus, who gave us the Lord's Prayer as the model for all our praying, the early Christians always uttered the Amen, the "So-be-it," through Jesus himself. Jesus became the guarantor of the prayer.

When the apostle Paul wrote the early chapters of the book we call II Corinthians, he was apparently responding to a feeling among some of the people of Corinth that he had not dealt forthrightly with them about some of his travel plans. "Was I vacillating when I wanted to do this?" he asked.

Do I make my plans like a worldly man, ready to say Yes and No at once? As surely as God is faithful, our word to you has not been Yes and No. For the Son of God, Jesus Christ, whom we preached among you, Silvanus and Timothy and I, was not Yes and No; but in him it is always Yes. For all the promises of God find their Yes in him. That is why we utter the Amen through him, to the glory of God. (II Corinthians 1:17-20)

This marked a great difference between the Christian and Jewish use of the word "Amen." The Jews pronounced the word as a liturgical response, as a word of personal ratification, as an exclamation of praise. But the Christians went farther, and said it with the sense that it was more powerful than any word spoken in their own names.

In fact, the early Christians went even farther than this, and identified Christ himself as the Amen, as the one causing the prayer to come true. When John was inspired to write the book of Revelation, on the island of Patmos, he saw the risen Lord in a vision. Jesus was clothed in gold. His voice, said John, was "like the sound of many waters," and his face was "like the sun shining in full strength." Jesus told him to write letters to each of the seven churches of Asia Minor. When he came to the seventh, the church at Laodicea, Jesus commanded him to write: "The words of the Amen, the faithful and true witness, the beginning of God's creation" (Revelation 3:14). Jesus himself was speaking as the Amen, the one making God's kingdom to come on earth!

What does this mean? What indeed but that

each and every time we pray the Lord's Prayer, we must, when we come to the end and speak the little word "Amen," remember that we do not speak it alone, but through Christ, the Son of the living God, whose resurrection from the dead is the promise that all the things for which we pray—kingdom, daily bread, forgiveness, and endurance—shall be granted.

Our situation is like that of Dr. V. P. Patterson, a retired missionary doctor to China, when he was a young man with no money for an education. The dean of a medical school called him in and gave him the address of an important businessman in Alabama, a cotton broker, who wanted to help a medical student. Young Patterson went to see him. The man sat behind a big desk in an enormous office. There were six telephones on the desk. After a brief conversation, the man reached in a desk drawer and took out a checkbook with fifty checks in it. He went through and signed every one of them. "Here," he said, "cash one of these every month for what you need."

Only one time, said Dr. Patterson, did the amount of the checks ever vary. That was on the occasion when there was an explosion in the laboratory and his only suit of clothes was ruined. The man wrote him a note and asked, "Why was your check greater this time?" Patterson sent him a photograph of the wrecked laboratory and a newspaper account of the explosion, together with a copy of the bill for his new suit. A few days later he received a postcard from the man saying, "I'm sorry I asked."

"I could never have become a doctor if it hadn't

been for that man," Dr. Patterson told me. "I couldn't get credit that way with anyone else— even my own family."

When we pray the Lord's Prayer through Jesus as the great Amen, it is as though we were writing a check on one who has already signed for us and whose credit is good. We are praying through one who has known us and loved us and given his life for us, and God cannot refuse him, for he is God's beloved Son.

"Amen."

It is a small word, but it is a powerful word. The early Christians knew what they were doing when they added it to the Lord's Prayer, for it is more than a mere liturgical response. It is a statement of faith and a shout of acclamation. And Aunt Susie knew what she was doing when she encouraged her preacher by shouting "Amen" and "Yes, Jesus." The Amen means it will be done through Jesus, and that is why we pray the prayer in the first place.